Dad's Stories
And Other Tales of
Balderdash

Dad's Stories
And Other Tales of
Balderdash

Thomas Dominick

XULON PRESS

Xulon Press
2301 Lucien Way #415
Maitland, FL 32751
407.339.4217
www.xulonpress.com

Unless otherwise indicated, Scripture quotations taken from the King
James Version (KJV) – *public domain*.

Printed in the United States of America.

Paperback ISBN-13: 978-1-6312-9241-5

Hardcover ISBN-13: 978-1-6312-9242-2
Dust Jacket ISBN-13: 978-1-6312-9243-9

Ebook ISBN-13: 978-1-6312-9244-6

DEDICATION

THIS BOOK IS dedicated to the greatest children a father could have. Stephen, Katherine, and Sara, this book I leave as my love and legacy for you.

Acknowledgements

A SPECIAL THANKS TO Jim Matthes, Erica Coulter, Gregory Dixon, and all the others at Xulon Press who made this book possible. You turned a vision that I imagined into a reality. I am especially thankful to all my many friends and family who touched my life profoundly throughout the years. I wouldn't have been able to accomplish this without you.

TABLE OF CONTENTS

Chapter One

THE FUDGE INCIDENT

I STILL SAVOR TODAY the smells that drifted away from Mom's kitchen. Often, there were warm cookies or a pie cooling when my sister Becky and I returned from school. One day, Mom made a pan of her intensely delicious fudge and placed it atop the TV set with explicit instructions not to touch it—I ask you, what six-year-old child can resist that sort of temptation? NOT ME!

Shortly after Mom left the room, a dilemma occurred. I decided she wouldn't notice if a piece of that fudge was missing; after all, there was a whole plate of it. "Just This One Time Won't Hurt," the little voice in my head was saying. As you might have guessed, "Just This One Time" turned into "This Time It's Too Good To Stop." When mom discovered the heist, there was BIG trouble in MY camp—and to top it off, NO DESSERT! Yes, sugar and me...we go way back.

Chapter Two

HERE, KITTY KITTY

DAD LIKED BEING a prankster if the opportunity arose. His skills were usually harmless, and he did them quite well… most of the time. Once, he accidently lit a man's beard on fire as he attempted to prank him with a cigarette lighter. Fortunately, the man's beard was only singed, and the fire snuffed out immediately.

Being a true fan of the TV show Gunsmoke Dad liked one of the female characters named "Miss Kitty." My parents were still newlyweds when they adopted a cocker spaniel puppy. Dad named her Miss Kitty after his favorite character, but they shortened her name to "Kitty."

Most people would be happy naming their dog a suitable name like Sam or Spot. I can even accept Fido or Rover. Not dad; he named the dog Kitty! I can picture him calling her and saying, "Here Kitty," then seeing this cute cocker spaniel sprint from the yard into the house. Anyone can imagine how confusing this would be to a young child, as Mom and Dad were about to see.

Both were going about their day when there was a knock at the door. The neighbor living next to them asked if she could come in and speak about her problem. With a worried look, she began to explain she didn't want to poke her nose into their business, but there was an issue that needed some attention…describing how her five-year-old son became very confused after seeing Kitty running into the house, asking if they could possibly consider changing her name. Knowing my dad, Kitty kept her name.

Chapter Three
IT'S FOR THE BIRDS

OUR BACKYARD WAS a place where we gathered for many picnics. Usually, on the weekend, Mom would make a cold meal consisting of tuna salad with a side of Jell-O® and potato salad. This was about the only time I wouldn't complain about eating fish! After dinner, Mom cleared the table and washed the dishes while Dad entertained Becky and me.

Sometimes, Mom would sit on our back steps and read to us. My favorite story was "THE BEAR STORY," written by James Whitcomb Riley, an epic tale told from a young boy's point of view about hunting a bear. I listened closely as mom read aloud, trying to imagine I was the boy in the story, laughing and giggling as she made silly voices acting out the characters.

David and Helen were the names of dad's parents, the only grandparents I knew growing up. "Big Daddy," as we affectionately called him, owned a fish and poultry market and loved watching baseball on TV. Back in his youth, he pitched for a minor league team with aspirations of playing professionally. He was good with his craft and well on his way until a torn rotator cuff in his pitching arm ended his dream.

We called our grandmother Helen "Grandma," a sweet Southern Belle from the state of Alabama. Each morning, she would start early preparing a farm-style breakfast for her family—a meal which included bacon and eggs, grits, and homemade biscuits, served warm with butter and dark molasses. I remember sitting on her lap with her arms cradled around me. It really was a treat to be present at her table.

Mom's father was named John; he lived in Indiana with his second wife Esther, whom he married after his wife Rebecca passed away. His second marriage happening before I was born. When I was two years old, John passed away. Mom and Dad left me in the guardianship of Grandma while they went to Indiana to attend his funeral.

It was time for lunch on that pleasantly warm and sunny afternoon. A perfect day to eat in the backyard. I remember peanut butter and jelly sandwiches with an ice-cold glass of milk being served. Getting a two-year-old to sit down to eat isn't easy, especially one with other ambitions. Chasing a group of crows was more fun! I'd send them to scurry away and watch as they circled around to land again.

Grandma was calling me to come and sit with her, but I wanted no part of it. "What if you eat a bite then throw one to the birds?" she suggested. That did the trick! I sat pronto and began eating. After taking a bite of sandwich, I'd throw a piece to the birds. Immediately, everyone was scrambling to get their share, as if they hadn't eaten in weeks! It was entertaining to see them squabble and compete. I don't know who ate more that afternoon, them or me, but it sure was memorable.

Chapter Four

HURRICANE HIJINKS

IN THE LATE summer of 1960, our dad accepted a job that required him to be away from home for an extended period. A decision was made to temporally relocate with him, settling into a small garden-style apartment near Tampa, on Florida's west coast.

A cluster of rain clouds drifted away from Africa, gaining strength as they moved westward. Hurricane Donna was born from there and became the most powerful tropical storm of the year. After visiting the islands in the Caribbean and Cuba, Donna made a direct track to us in Florida, arriving with all her fury.

In many instances, exterior doors in Florida are designed to swing outward to comply with building codes. In the event of a hurricane, the winds would push against the door and lessen the chance of it failing structurally. Our apartment had doors with louvered glass windows that opened to the outside. Next to the rear door on the exterior walkway was a heavy metal canister that held propane gas for cooking. Fearing the tank might break away or explode after a huge gust of wind blew it over, Dad quickly reacted and exited through the back door.

My young mind interpreted things in ways far differently from reality. The howling wind and heavy rains were endless, and seeing my dad exit our home in a very unusual way while all this was happening seemed odd to me.

Mom and I were just feet away when we saw the head of our family go sailing out into the storm with the door he barely opened. A large gale had pushed its way into the space that he'd created and pulled him away. Curiously, I looked up and asked, "Mommy, why did Daddy throw the door away?" Luckily escaping from serious injury, Dad was able to upright the tank and nail the door back in place with help from a few neighbors.

The storm produced severe damage and no electricity for a week. Fortunately, there was gas for cooking. I remember Becky and I taking bubble baths outside in our swimsuits in a kiddie pool that Mom and Dad purchased. We thought it a fun way to get clean, but I'm sure our parents would say that it was being resourceful.

Chapter Five

MEETING MR. BONES

MY FIFTH CHRISTMAS morning was spent at our grand-parent's house. We were staying there while they were away visiting family for the holidays. After opening our gifts, I asked permission to go next door and visit with my cousins. I wanted to go and see all their exciting presents. As I exited the back door, I saw an unfamiliar dog running directly at me, and it looked mean. Terrified, I screamed and ran back into the house. Little did I know, this pup was just as afraid of me because I was too busy to notice that we were running in opposite directions. Mom held on to her amusement as she peered through the window.

What I saw running toward me was a Christmas gift my cousins had received. His name was Mr. Bones, an English Bulldog approximately a year old. To a young lad such as myself, "Bones" (as we referred to him) looked fierce and mean. He sported the typical pushed-in type of face of his breed, drooping jowls and a tongue that sat between two bottom front teeth protruding from his lower jaw. Bones may have looked the part, but his personality gave him away, a gentle soul that would never hurt anyone.

Bones loved chasing cars. I'm guessing every dog has their one vice they can't seem to break; it must have been a sport to him. I remember seeing him aggressively chasing any car that dared passing his domain. Charging and barking, he would head down the street moving as fast as his short legs would carry him. Minutes later, he'd return home completely exhausted.

One afternoon, Mom took the car to run a few errands, and Bones started chasing her. Suddenly, there was a loud bump at the front fender. Mr. Bones met the business end of her vehicle. Immediately, Mom stopped the car. Looking back and seeing Bones laying in the street made her visibly shaken thinking he was dead. After a minute or so, Mr. Bones amazingly woke up and trotted away as if nothing happened. He was one tough bulldog!

Chapter Six

SCHNAPPS AND THE POT ROAST

ONE EVENING, AFTER sitting down to eat, there was a knock at the front door. A teenaged neighbor was there holding the cutest dashund puppy in need of a good home. It was close to my birthday, and I begged to have her as my birthday present. Reluctantly, Mom and Dad gave in to a decision they ultimately regretted. Being a German breed, we named her Schnapps.

From the very beginning, Schnapps was a handful of trouble. In a short time, she grew from being sweet and cute into Dogzilla. Her welcome mat was wearing thin. This became more evident after moving into a new home our parents built.

I couldn't figure why this fifteen-pound pup caused so many problems. Schnapps was very spiteful when left at home, destroying anything available. Magazines and newspapers didn't stand a chance. Her last act of disapproval was leaving her personal business on the carpeting next to the linoleum floor! It was as if she knew it was harder to clean up the mess from the carpet than it was to clean the linoleum. I commend my parents for putting up with her for as long as they did, but the pot roast incident—that was the final straw!

Our dad was six feet and two inches tall, and his name was Newt. "Newt the Brute," we used to call him, but he was far from that. He was a hard worker, a good provider, and a gentle giant of a man—except when someone or something interfered with his dinner.

Once again, we just sat down for dinner when there was a knock at the door. Everyone left the table to see who was there. Schnapps, not missing an opportunity to seize the moment, climbed up on the table to get her fair share of the pot roast Mom lovingly made for dinner.

We returned to the dining room, horrified to find our beloved canine front paws and face deep in the platter, chowing down on OUR dinner! At that point, time seemed to slow down. I remember Dad letting out a yell that you could hear in the next county while applying a potent slap to Schnapp's hindquarters. Spinning off the table, she must have thought she was on one of those celebrity dancing shows, pirouetting and landing a perfect ten before scampering off to hide. As for the pot roast, it was taken off the menu.

Not long afterward, Schnapps left another of her presentations in the house. Hearing Dad yell, "I'm not going to let a ten-cent dog ruin our new home!" I sensed her days in our home were numbered. Later that day, Schnapps disappeared.

It was suggested Becky and I go spend an afternoon at the movies…notified of Schnapp's disappearance after returning home, Mom and Dad telling us Schnapps accidently escaped through the garage door.

Although never admitting guilt to anything, I have my doubts. It would be several years before another pet crossed the threshold of our home.

Chapter Seven

THE ONE I WISH HAD GOTTEN AWAY!

AS A YOUNG boy, I was excited to go fishing with my dad. We'd get up early and gather our things, then head out in hopes of landing "The Big One." Sometimes, we would meet up with my uncles and a couple of cousins then head down to the bay, planning for a successful day.

Upon arrival, we would rent a small boat and set off in search of our prey. It doesn't matter who found the spot, but there was a special place where we would drop anchor and the fish were almost begging us to catch them.

Around noon, we would return to the dock with our haul. Dad and my uncles would dress the fish and place them on ice. After a quick bite to eat, we would return to repeat the process.

When we got home, the bountiful catch was divided; Dad kept his share in a garage freezer. That's when the fun ended! I enjoyed fishing and didn't mind cleaning and dressing them. When it came to the eating part—I'll pass! There was no way I was about to let any of it pass through my lips!

Mom spelled her name the same as Bette Davis, her favorite actress. Knowing her way around the kitchen,

Mom could make a gourmet meal out of leftovers. I would never doubt her cooking abilities except when it came to a plate of fish. There was absolutely nothing she could do to make it palatable enough for me to eat. As soon as my nose caught the first scent molecules drifting through the air, I knew there was going to be an argument—one that wouldn't end well for me!

Dad's rule was you had to eat what's served and finish everything on your plate. My parents would say, "Think of all of the starving children that don't have anything to eat that would love to have your dinner."

My response: "How does finishing my dinner help any of the starving children become fed?" The answer to my question was followed up with a sharp negative response and a smack for talking back! When fish was on the menu, I had a choice to eat or go hungry. Leaving the table, I chose to go hungry.

After serving a large dose of indigestion, I was sent to my room. When dinner was finished, I could rejoin the family. Eagerly, I would greet a peanut butter and jelly sandwich Mom left for me. It's funny how your tastes in food change as you mature. As I became older, I started to enjoy a variety of seafood dishes and continue to enjoy them to this day.

Chapter Eight

LIFE IS A BEACH

GROWING UP NEAR the beach might be the envy of many. For me, not so much. The young neighbor that came to our doorstep carrying the puppy we called Schnapps was named *Ellen. Occasionally, she would stop and offer to take Becky and me to the beach for an afternoon of fun. Her way of having fun would profoundly change me and the way I felt about the ocean for many years.

Ellen showed up one afternoon to take me to the beach. For some reason, Becky stayed home that day. We arrived to claim our spot near the water's edge. I stayed close, not venturing far from her sight. After a while, Ellen asked if I wanted to get into the water with her. I agreed and held tightly to her hand as we headed toward the breakers. I was approximately six years old and hadn't learned to swim. The waves were breaking a little rough and were up to her waist when she stopped to place me on her hip. The water was getting deeper as we continued, and I was scared. Ellen's feet were barely touching the sand beneath her when she stated, "I want you to swim to shore!" Without warning, Ellen let go of me and stepped away. "Start swimming!" she said. Survival instincts took over, and I began to paddle frantically. Within minutes, I was back on land with Ellen trailing closely behind. Sobbing through uncontrollable tears, I pleaded for her to take me home. From that day forward, I declined any requests that involved going to the beach. My toes wouldn't touch a sandy shore again until my teenage years.

My friends *Dan and Perry enjoyed hitting the waves quite often. I would excuse myself whenever they asked me to join them, still haunted by my last ocean experience. That all changed when I discovered the beach was a happening place to meet girls! By now, I learned to swim but stubbornly sat on my towel, determined not to get in the water. Dan and Perry would visit a reef not far from shore and catch fish for Dan's aquarium. I chose not to participate in their big adventure as they donned their gear. In their possession was an instrument that resembled a large syringe used for catching fish and an old inner tube lined with fishnet. I watched as they entered through the breakers and disappeared.

They returned carrying many beautifully colored fish, describing all the amazing things they'd seen. I was intrigued but still hesitant to join them. Eventually, my curiosity outweighed my fear, and I decided to participate in their fun—after watching a very scary movie.

One Friday evening, Dan, Perry, and I went to see a newly released film about a large shark terrorizing a popular tourist resort. Many scenes were graphic, and the intensity kept us on the edge of our seats. Afterwards, Dan and Perry invited me to join them for an early morning trek to the reef. Reluctantly, I told them yes.

Early the next morning, we stood on the beach with our gear ready to go. Though terrified, I convinced myself it was too late to opt out now. As we made our way to the reef, my fears were replaced by pure astonishment. Never had I seen such beauty.

Less than twenty-four hours ago, I had witnessed a large ocean predator devour everything excluding my popcorn. Today, I'm navigating an amazing undersea world with my friends, confidently aware I had overcome my anxiety and fear of swimming in the ocean.

Chapter Nine

KEEPING WITH A TRADITION

WHEN MY PARENTS designed and built a custom-made home, all that Mom wanted was a fireplace and a house to surround it. Mom was a traditionalist in every way when it came to the holidays. The day after Thanksgiving, boxes were brought from the attic filled with Christmas decor ready for placement. Soon, the tree was illuminated with many colored lights. Ornaments old and new adorned almost every branch, and the fragrance of a freshly cut fir tree drifted throughout the room. Let the celebration begin!

The first Christmas in our new home was very memorable, not so much for the gifts we received. What made this day memorable was the outside temperature—it was HOT! Living at the far end of the southernmost US state, one cannot expect to have an abundance of cold weather, even on Christmas Day.

Before any gifts were opened, Dad had a pot of coffee brewing. As for Mom, her request was to have the fireplace lit. It wasn't long before we felt the heat—literally! We all were very thankful that our a/c unit was in good working order. Dad adjusted the thermostat to the lowest setting, and it took a while to achieve a comfortable environment. As for keeping that tradition, we skipped it the next year!

Chapter Ten

DAD AND THE RACCOON

MY COUSIN CAROL was given a baby raccoon for her sixth birthday. She named him Bandit, and Dad thought he was adorable. Becky and I tried to convince Mom that a baby raccoon would be an excellent Christmas present for our dad. Naturally, Mom was down for it and played along.

Ten days before Christmas, Becky and I arrived from school and discovered the garage doors were locked and newspaper was covering the windows. Mom told us this area was off limits. It was then I was convinced Dad was getting a raccoon for Christmas! Mom just smiled and went on about her business as usual.

Becky and I were out of our minds with anticipation when Christmas finally arrived. Bursting through the garage door, we were expecting to see a baby raccoon waiting for us...but found a pool table instead! The disappointment of not seeing a raccoon was quickly overtaken by thought of having a pool table. *How cool is that?! My friends are really going to be jealous of me,* I thought. I doubt they were all that jealous, but one thing for sure, Mom and Dad knew where we were playing most of the time. Gee, I wonder if that was good planning on their part?

Chapter Eleven

HAIR TODAY, GONE TOMORROW

JAZMINE* WAS IN my third-grade class and as smart as she was cute! A quiet girl with blue eyes and long, wavy blonde hair ending at her waistline. You might think someone that pretty sitting in front of me would be a good thing—not through the eyes of this eight-year-old. It was a curse!

The problem was her hair! She habitually leaned backwards, pushing those golden locks onto my desk, usually striking me in the face. I asked several times that she move her desk farther away from mine, but her strands would eventually return.

One afternoon, I noticed a thumbtack next to my shoe. Picking it up, I waited for the next opportunity to end this hairy harassment. If any of those strands came flying my way, I'd be waiting. It didn't take long before they were back invading my space! What happened next, I'm not proud to share. I took that thumbtack and pushed it deep into the desktop, trapping about a half-inch wide swath of her hair, then waited... When it came time for her to get up from her seat, my plan unfolded. Without sharing any of the ugly details, I think you'll get the picture. My reward was a quick escort to the principal's office for a couple of reminders on the rear this type of behavior wasn't acceptable. As far as Jazmine, her desk was moved far away from mine. You might say it was a winning situation for both of us.

Chapter Twelve

School Daze

THE TWO THINGS I enjoyed about grade school were recess and the final bell. I wasn't interested in any lessons being taught, and my grades were suffering. One afternoon, my teacher told me stay after class, asking me to hand deliver a sealed note to my parents. I knew I'd be in deep trouble if Mom and Dad saw it and things would get messy.

Carefully, I started opening the note as I walked home and was horrified by what it said. The note stated I wasn't paying attention and causing disruptions in the classroom. It went on to say that a parent-teacher conference was necessary because I hadn't turned in any of my homework assignments.

I could feel my chest tighten, along with a lump forming in my throat. I knew if my parents caught wind of this, it wouldn't be good. I decided to make the note disappear by crumpling it up and leaving it in a wastebasket.

When I got home, Mom asked about my day at school and if I had any homework. I replied, "School was okay, and I didn't have homework."

After changing clothes and a quick snack, I was off to meet up with friends. "Be home by dinnertime," I heard Mom say as I bolted out the front door.

After a few hours of playing, I came bounding through the door ready for dinner. Mom and Dad were seated at the table, looking as if someone had died. My heart sank. "Where's the note your teacher sent home with you?" My dad asked.

"What note?" I replied. From there, things deteriorated fast! Apparently, my teacher called to see if I had delivered her message. I discounted the fact she'd do a follow-up phone call and was sent back to find the note. After reading it, my parents revoked most privileges until my assignments were completed and the grades improved. I learned the hard way two valuable lessons that day: never try and outsmart your parents, and never underestimate the follow-up phone call from a teacher!

Chapter Thirteen

BULLY FOR ME

JEFFERY* WAS MY friend in middle school, or so I thought. I don't know how or why, but something suddenly caused him to think otherwise.

One Friday after school, I was informed that Jeffrey was planning to be at our house on Saturday morning to pick a fight with me. My parents believed that fighting was a bad thing and discouraged me from doing so. I was taught not to look for trouble and to be the "Bigger" person. "Just walk away from it," they would say. I was wondering how I would do that if the trouble came looking for me. I barely slept, wondering what I would do if Jeffrey were to show up.

At ten o'clock the next morning, there was a knock at the front door. Jeffrey was there, true to his word. Becky ran and opened the door, letting me know that I had a visitor.

Stepping outside and closing the door behind me, I asked why he was standing at our front door. He replied that he wanted to start a fight with me. I asked why, and he couldn't figure out the reason, just that he wanted me to fight with him. When I asked if he would rather watch TV instead of fighting, he said yes, much to my surprise.

I was overcome with a huge sense of relief having averted a major conflict. Within minutes, we were sitting on the floor in front of the TV watching cartoons. It would be the last time Jeffery and I would spend time together. Mom said that it was incredible how I was able to convince him not to fight and I should become a diplomat. Maybe someday I will win the Nobel Prize when I figure out how to obtain world peace…

Chapter Fourteen

THE SCIENCE PROJECT

PERRY AND I were inside of his dad's workshop scanning through the pages of his army manual. One item that captured our attention would soon provide plenty of "Bang" for our buck. Immediately, we started working on fulfilling our plan.

Perry's mom obliged by taking us to the hobby store. Our excuse, we needed to buy a few items for a school project. Little did she know about our scheming plan, and we weren't about to divulge otherwise.

Back home, we began working like mad chemists, and soon the ill-advised project was finished. Hastily, we made our way to a nearby lot to complete our mission. After finding the perfect spot, we buried our device in the sand. Placing a lit cigarette at the ignition point would give us time to flee the area, hopefully without being seen. Minutes passed like hours, tempting us to return and check on our handiwork. Finally, the anticipation was over as every window in the neighborhood rattled. Perry and I were pleased with our efforts and couldn't wait to see the results. Standing in disbelief, we gazed at the large crater carved into the ground. Deciding not to loiter, we returned to Perry's front yard.

Perry's mom met us, wondering if we knew anything about the thunderous event that had violently shook her windows. Trying our best to hide our expressions, we told her no. I'm guessing she possibly knew we were guilty of something but couldn't prove it. The irresponsibility of our actions could have ruined many lives. It took a few guardian angels and a miracle to prevent that from happening.

Chapter Fifteen

TODAY, WE'RE GOING TO STUDY...THIS!

IN THE NINTH grade, we studied Earth Science. Our teacher Mr. *Robinson would enter the classroom carrying a long wooden pointer in his left hand while pulling down a large rollup map with his right. He must have practiced this move for weeks, stepping from his office, sweeping his arm across his body, always landing on the subject of study. This daily ritual continued until I had an idea...a devilishly good deed that changed the way he approached the map, at least until I graduated.

Sneaking in before class, I cautiously made my way to the map. The very one he pulled every day. Making sure no one would see me, I began unrolling the picture, knowing I had mere seconds to finish and get seated.

The bell rang, and class began. Mr. R. entered the room on cue and proceeded to the map, gave it a tug, and swung his pointer. "Today We're Going to Study This!" Before he could realize what was happening, the class erupted into mass hysteria. Looking back, he got the picture—the picture of a centerfold from a girly magazine I had skillfully taped to the map. Realizing this, his face turned beet red, and he was clearly shocked to see the picture of a provocatively dressed lady staring back at him. Surely, this was the last thing on his mind. After reclaiming his composure, the picture was taken down and class resumed. From that day forward, he would cautiously pull the map, always aware there could be another surprise waiting for him. Finally, I confessed it was me who pranked him on that fateful day. Surprisingly, he wasn't angry or upset, and we had a good laugh, although at the time, he remained a professional and didn't show his amusement.

Chapter Sixteen

IT'S SNOW JOKE

"YEA, RIGHT!" WAS my reaction that Wednesday when Mom's phone call awoke me from a deep and peaceful slumber. It was 8:30 in the morning, having been home a couple of hours after working all night. I could hear the excitement in her voice as she said, "Look outside, it's snowing!" telling me to get up from my warm and cozy bed and look. So, I did. On January 19, 1977, it was snowing in South Florida, the home of oranges and palm trees! Miami, Florida, never heard the word "snow" mentioned in the forecast in eighty-seven years! Not since officially keeping records in 1890.

It was colder in Miami, Florida, than in Anchorage, Alaska, according to the National Weather Service. Although the amount of snow was light and not enough to cover the grass, it was still snow! I peered through sleepy eyes to see a swirl of flakes collecting on the colder surfaces. My car had magically transformed from powder blue to white in the span of two hours! Classes were cancelled as schools observed their first official "snow day." Farther north, higher amounts of snow were measured in parts of the state, enough to cover the ground. Limbs bearing ice-covered fruit were drooping to the ground with oranges hard as baseballs. It might take another eighty-seven years for such an event to happen, but one thing's for certain—it won't be in my lifetime.

Chapter Seventeen

FOR THE LOVE OF FOOTBALL

ONE OF MY fondest memories was watching football with my dad. Sunday afternoons were special as we excitedly waited for the game to start. It was 1970, the beginning of a new era for the local pro football team having few victories of late. A new coach promised to turn them in to champions. With our anticipations running high, we hoped he was good at keeping his word. By season's end, this amazing team was in the playoffs. Two years later, they were undefeated champions. I'd say this coach kept his word.

*Ron was an acquaintance that hosted a sports radio show. He'd send me with a list of questions for the players and coaches about their upcoming game. Back in studio, we'd edit and play the best clips on the air. Being a huge fan, I was fortunate to get an opportunity that others didn't, the ability of having a close connection with the team.

Shortly after the millennium of 2000, I moved to Oregon and was hired by a livery service that shuttled players back and forth from the airport to a prestigious golfing club that catered to the rich and famous. Weather conditions were ideal and closely resembled those in Scotland without forgoing the trip.

One afternoon, as I was loading clubs, I noticed "Miami, Florida" written on one of the tags. I was confident there would be some interesting conversation on this trip! Shortly after the bags were loaded, we departed. I started by introducing myself and letting them know I grew up in Miami. Someone asked why I was living so far away from home. I responded by saying I moved to Oregon because of the opportunity and a desire to live there.

From the back of the van came another question. "Do you follow any sports teams?" I eagerly said, "YES!" I was a huge fan of the football team from their area. Then another question wanting my opinion of the man who made them champions two years in a row. I answered by saying I thought he (the coach) could almost walk on water, according to his fans. For the remainder of the trip, our conversation mainly focused on living in Florida and things we enjoyed about living there.

Upon our arrival, I was directed across the tarmac to a twin-engine commuter plane that was fueled and ready. I pulled the van nearby and parked. After helping my passengers exit, I began loading the plane with their belongings. As I went to grab one of the bags, I noticed it had this famous coach's name stitched on the socks covering his clubs. One of the golfers noticed my surprised expression and pointed to Don Shula, the very man I interviewed so many years ago. I had no idea he was in the van listening to my every word! I completed the task of transferring everything into the plane and wished them a safe trip home. I stepped into the van and began to pull away when one of the men signaled for me to stop. Thinking I forgot something, I stopped. Walking up to my window, he said that Mr. Shula appreciated my professionalism and placed a crisp one-hundred-dollar bill in my hand. That really made my day!

*Author's Note: My first interaction with Coach Don Shula came when I was fifteen years old. My Dad and I went to see to a pre-season scrimmage that the team was holding. Afterwards, Coach Shula and his players met the attending fans signing autographs. I was fortunate enough to meet him and get his autograph. On May 4th, 2020 Coach Shula died peacefully at his home. He will be remembered as the winningest pro football coach in history. I will remember him as a great leader of men that gave totally of himself in everything that he did. He was truly one of a kind.

Chapter Eighteen

DEUTERONOMY 1:7

OUR MOM HAILED from the Hoosier state of Indiana. A series of unfortunate events prompted her to leave, hoping for a new beginning in Florida. A chance meeting after stopping to purchase a tank of gas would be that beginning. There was someone waiting to fill her heart with love, someone who would eventually become our dad.

He engineered a plan, hoping to bring her back for a second time by craftily leaving an oilcan and spout in place atop the vehicle's engine. The plan worked; a few days later, Mom returned. They were destined to fall in love and married on December 18, 1954, after a six-month courtship.

Mom and Dad were blissfully together nearly twenty-three years. On July 30, 1977, Dad unexpectedly passed away at the age of fifty-two. His sudden departure began a chain of events that profoundly changed our family. Dad's passing left a big void, especially for Mom. I think she started dying the minute he did, surviving on coffee and cigarettes for the next nine years. I could never replace the man who was her rock and cornerstone, but ready or not, I had to step up and become a man.

Becky started fall classes at the University of Tennessee in Knoxville, which left Mom and me to carry on with our daily lives. I tried to be supportive, but there were days we held each other and cried endless tears for him.

Mom's sister, Pat, and husband, Tom, were living in New Jersey in a stunning glass and brick home he designed and built. Mom was invited to live with them until she could find her own place. I was surprised when Mom revealed the only reason for living in the Sunshine State was her love for our dad. After much consideration, Mom's decision was final; New Jersey would be her new home.

The night before we left, I laid in bed, wondering if we were making the right decision. I believe that God speaks to us if we'll only stop to listen. I remember hearing a voice in my dreams telling me to look at Deuteronomy 1:7. I awoke and found the passage in my Bible. The opening line read, "It's time to break camp and move on." Putting my fears away, I knew we were making the right decision.

On January 29, 1979, we left our family home of thirteen years for the last time. A total of 4,881 days passed since moving in on September 18, 1965. I was sad to leave but looking forward to joining Perry now living in Tennessee, working on his cousins 360-acre horse farm.

The following day, we arrived in Tennessee. After unloading my belongings and a good night's rest, Mom and I were on the road bound for New Jersey. I enjoyed spending a few days visiting with relatives and helped Mom get settled. Now it was time to begin a new chapter away from home and family.

Chapter Nineteen

OH, MY ACHING BACK!

LIVING ON A farm that raised thoroughbred quarter horses was quite a new experience. Having grown up in suburbia, it took a while before I adjusted to the physical labor. My sore muscles were a constant reminder of that! Eventually, I managed, but the routine of getting up before dawn and finishing long after sundown was never easy.

*Mark was in charge of the farm's daily operations. Every morning, Perry and I started our day by taking care of the horses. Next, it was time to clean the barn. After raking out the stalls and applying a fresh layer of sawdust, it was time to start working.

Believe me, there were chores galore to keep us busy year-round. Plenty of hours were spent cutting acres of grass across the Tennessee farmland. After a few days, the hay was dry enough to bale. Perry and I would load the seventy-five-pound haybales onto a flatbed trailer Mark was towing with a tractor. It was quite a workout. When we completed stacking a load, we'd return to the barn and place it in the hayloft. This strenuous routine continued throughout the summer.

On one occasion, before my arrival, Perry told me he and Mark were in the field loading bales of hay. By day's end, not all of the bales were collected, with several acres needing completion. After finishing the evening chores, Perry returned home totally exhausted and fell asleep. Shortly after two in the morning, he was awakened by the phone; it was Mark. Rain was coming, and the remaining bales needed to be inside away from the weather. Mark and Perry spent the rest of the night saving what was left and finished shortly before the rain began falling. When the morning chores were done, Perry was granted a well-deserved day off.

Chapter Twenty

DAIRY DOWNER

IT WAS AROUND 6:00 p.m. on a typically hot summer's day. I was returning to the barn from a long day of mowing when the phone rang. A neighboring dairy farm needed help with the evening chores. Before I could mount a good defense as to why I shouldn't help, I was heading there!

I'd never seen a Holstein, let alone milked one, but ready or not, here I come. When I arrived, the milking process was running smoothly. That is...until I showed up. I would find out soon enough that milking a herd of seventy-five "lovely ladies" was going to be a challenge.

Any dairy farmer will tell you getting dirty is part of the job and not for the faint of heart. This farm was no different. I introduced myself to *Julie, who was wearing blue overalls splattered with whatever spews from the back end of a cow. She had the task of showing me the ropes of milking 101. For those of you unfamiliar with the milking process, here are a few basic terms. The place where the cows are milked is called the parlor, and you stand below them in the pit when they are milking. The heifers enter on each side of the pit in single file. After my brief introduction, it was time to get busy with the task at hand. I climbed into the pit feeling a bit anxious but eager to learn.

Julie showed me how to clean the udders with a sanitizing solution and the proper way to dry them. She attached the electric milking devices by placing one teat cup on each quarter of the udder. Almost instantly, the milk began flowing. Now it was my turn. Julie helped as I placed my hands into the pail of warm solution, explaining again how important it was to thoroughly clean the udders and why it was necessary to properly dry them. I nervously pulled the rag out from the cleaning solution and began wiping the area as shown. Standing eye level with the belly of a 1300-pound bovine was quite an experience, especially when her dirty, wet tail hit me in the face!

There are four cups, each with a hose that connects with the milk claw. The claw is round and roughly the size of a tennis ball. The milk passes from the cups into the claw, where it's drawn out by a vacuum hose. From there, it flows into a refrigerated holding tank for later pickup.

Now that I graduated from milking 101, it was time for milking 102. I watched as Julie placed the claw in the palm of her right hand and easily attached the cups to the four protrusions extending from the tightly swollen bag. "See, that was easy enough," she said and handed me a claw. Little did we know that a near disaster was about to happen.

I placed the claw in my right hand as shown, the four hoses draping on each side. As I attempted to put the first cup in place, "Ole Bessy" decided that she wasn't having any part of that! Without warning, she gave a sharp blow to my right arm, sending the claw flying away from my grasp. Never in my life had I experienced such pain! Immediately, I heard nothing! There was total silence, only an occasional bellow from one of the four-legged patrons. What had been running like a well-oiled machine was at an abrupt HALT!

After determining nothing was broken, I discovered the claw went directly into the pail of cleaner. The four cups were eagerly drawing sanitizer into the line. Julie immediately pushed the EMERGENCY STOP button just in time to prevent a catastrophe. Fortunately, just a minimal amount of milk was lost. After flushing out the affected parts, normal operations continued, and we finished without any more incidents. My first day of training as a dairy farmer may have started out roughly, but I was willing to learn. It wasn't long before I was able to attach and remove the cups effortlessly, hopefully without the risk of being kicked.

Chapter Twenty-One

FAMILY REUNION

AFTER NEARLY FOUR years of farm life, it was time to move on. Becky graduated from college and was living close to Mom in New Jersey. Although I never imagined living there, I decided it was time to join them and reunite the family.

Waking to a dreary and cold day didn't help lighten the mood that morning. My leaving was bittersweet, sharing both excitement and sadness in my departure. Perry wished me well as we said our goodbyes, then I drove away. Staring at my rearview mirror, I watched as the big red barn slowly disappeared from sight. The next chapter in my life had begun. Winding my way through freezing rain and narrow country roads, I eventually reached the interstate and began my northward trek.

As the miles passed, the day grew dark and colder. Freezing rain changed to snow, and I was nowhere near civilization. Held tightly in the grip of a hellish winter storm, it would be several hours and a hundred triturate miles of road before I found refuge.

It was midnight when I saw a motel sign and pulled off the highway. The car was low on fuel, and I was thankful to find the last available space. After checking in to my room, I called Mom, letting her know I was safely off the road.

By morning, the storm departed, leaving me in its wake, clear skies and bright sunshine replacing the snowfall from the night before. I finished eating a hearty breakfast, then began to free my car from a deep coating of white powder. After quickly stopping at the gas pumps, I was on the road.

The early morning sun added luster to the glistening white canopy covering the landscape. The highway was clear except for an occasional briny mist sprayed across my windshield by passing vehicles.

It was early afternoon when I reached the toll plaza for the Pennsylvania Turnpike. I could feel the anticipation getting stronger as I drew closer to my destination, Mom's house. Four months earlier, we celebrated the day I reached a quarter century in Gatlinburg, Tennessee. Christmas was just days away, and I was looking forward to celebrating as a family for the first time in years.

New Jersey was quite an adjustment, a new lifestyle to which I was not accustomed. I eventually began a daily routine, staying with Mom until I could get a place of my own. Our family was finally together years after leaving our South Florida home.

In early January, I began working for a cable company as a service technician. The day usually began with a cup of hot coffee and a group of people waiting for their daily assignments. In an adjacent room, three ladies worked in the billing and dispatch office. Occasionally, I would chat with Donna until it was time to start my day. Never could I imagine we'd find true love, but it happened one fate full afternoon.

It was on a Friday, March 5, 1982. I was the last tech to enter the building, as most everyone had left for the weekend. I made my way to the billing office to leave my paperwork and found Donna visibly upset after being rudely abused on the phone. Asking for a little time to calm down, she stated she'd be fine. All the planets must have aligned as I mustered the courage to ask if she wanted to join me for dinner—to my surprise, she said yes.

Within minutes, we're conversing over steaming bowls of French onion soup. Two hours seemed like two minutes. I thoroughly enjoyed her company, and it left me longing for more. When I got home, Mom was worried. I neglected to tell her I was stopping for a rendez-vous after work.

The weekend passed, and it was Monday again. I showed up for work with an extra anticipation of seeing Donna. I had to suppress my feelings because we were in a working environment; besides, I didn't know if her feelings were the same as mine. I was hoping they were.

We continued seeing each other but played it cool around the workplace. The company forbid office romances from blooming. If anyone discovered our secret, one of us would have to leave immediately. Eventually, we were exposed, so I volunteered. Within a couple of weeks, I was working at the local community college in the audio-visual department.

A few evenings a week, Donna stopped after work to enjoy one of Mom's home-cooked meals. We'd spend the evening chatting or watching TV. At ten o'clock, it was time for us to say our goodbyes for the night.

Each day, our love and commitment grew stronger. We were at Mom's one evening when I asked Donna how she felt about getting married. Her reply: "Are you asking me to marry you?" I barely managed to squeak out the word "yes." All of a sudden, there was a huge lump in my throat that kept me from speaking. After five months of dating, I was sure of my intent.

I may have been ready to take the marital plunge, but Donna wasn't so sure. No man had ever asked her that question, and it caught her by surprise. It took a full week to reach her decision. The answer was crystal clear when she said yes! On May 7th of the following year, we were married.

Chapter Twenty-Two

AND THEN THERE WERE THREE

IT WAS COLD and snowy the day we arrived at the hospital to welcome the birth of our son, Stephen Newton-Paul Dominick, born January 3, 1985, at 3:34 in the afternoon. As I held him for the first time, I imagined my feelings being similar to my dad's when he first held me. I know he'd been honored and proud of his new namesake. Newton is a family name that was passed down for generations.

Being the first of anything had its advantages, especially when you're the first grandchild. There was no lack of love and attention from the two doting grandmothers and a host of family eager to greet him. I could never imagine the ultimate joy Donna and I shared when we became parents. Stephen was a product of the love that we shared, truly a gift from God.

Three days after his arrival, Stephen was brought home and given twenty-four hour undivided attention from two loving parents. For almost five years, the word "share" was rarely part of his vocabulary. That is…until hearing news that would change his world forever.

April 1989 brought some exciting news—we're expecting twins! Panic was the word best describing my feelings. Yes, I was happy and thrilled about the news, but the twins' part had me nervous. It was challenging to raise one child, but adding two more? How were we going to manage?

My aunt and uncle raised identical twin girls that were two years older than me. When I shared the news about us expecting our own pair of twins, my dear aunt burst out with laughter. When I asked her why she was laughing, she said we'd find out soon enough... and we did.

Katherine Marie and Sarah Elizabeth arrived by cesarean section on the morning of November 17, 1989, in the same hospital where their brother was born nearly five years earlier. Excited at the possibility of having a baby brother, Stephen was convinced that one of the babies was a boy; all he wanted was to be a big brother. His hopes were dashed when he learned it wouldn't happen.

The delivery was complete, and I was holding my two precious daughters. Donna and the babies were doing great, and it was time to deliver the good news. The first call was to my sister, Becky. Stephen was in her care while we were welcoming our new family members into the world. I told Stephen he was a big brother of two sisters, and there was total silence. It was if a ten-ton weight had fallen and crushed him. The next thing that I heard was a "click" as he hung up the phone. Immediately, I called back and asked for him. Becky stated he was too upset to speak with me, and I was to blame. No, I was just the messenger!

It took almost a week for Donna to recover from her surgery, but now it was time to go home. Stephen and I met her with the car just as the nurses were wheeling her through the double doors at the main entrance. With two swaddled football-sized bundles quietly sleeping in their car seats, we headed for home.

I quickly found out why my aunt was laughing when I phoned to let her know we were having twins. For the first few weeks, it seemed as if one or the other was crying, needing to be fed, or in need of a diaper change. It was all hands-on deck; even big brother Stephen chipped in. Eventually, things began to settle down, and a daily routine was established.

Katherine and Sarah were fraternal twins and could easily be identified by their features. Both had a distinctive cry and different colored hair. Katherine's hair was black as night, while Sara's was white as snow. I remember my aunt saying she had to tape her twins' names to the bottom of their feet in order to tell them apart.

One evening, after dinner, Donna was bathing the girls while Stephen supervised. When I finished in the kitchen, I helped to dress them for bed and tuck them in.

Stephen was as imaginative and inquisitive as any five-year-old. Most of the answers to his questions were simple, but the one he asked that evening I couldn't imagine him asking. "Daddy, can I send one back and get a baby brother?" His query was startling, and I could see his disappointment as he held on to any chance of having a brother. After explaining that his sisters were there to stay, he finally realized he couldn't trade either one for an upgraded model, as if they were a used car.

Chapter Twenty-Three

No Ma'am, You're Seeing Double!

I WAS AMAZED AT the number of times someone would stop and ask if Katherine and Sarah were twins! Both were dressed identically and sitting in their double stroller. I wanted to place a sign in front of them saying, "Don't ask, and yes, we are twins," but never did so. On one occasion, after a woman asked, I kiddingly pointed to Katherine and said that she was five years older, but smoking had stunted her growth. The lady looked shocked and walked away, shaking her head. I think she actually believed me!

Chapter Twenty-Four

OLIVER AND DRAKE

STEPHEN AND THE twins were mature enough to take on more responsibilities. Donna and I decided a pet would make a nice addition to our family. I'd heard from an acquaintance there was a dog in need, so we adopted Oliver and brought him home.

With a good-sized, fenced-in yard in which he and the kids could play, what could possibly go wrong? Did I mention Oliver was an English Sheepdog, a herding breed?

Stephen was ten years old, and the girls were five at the time. The only problem was Oliver! He thought Katherine and Sarah were sheep in need of herding. Obviously, this behavior would not be tolerated, and Oliver had to go. After making a few phone calls, I found a home for him in the country, where I'm sure he was much happier.

After the fiasco with Oliver, I wasn't sure if I wanted another dog—that is, until I met someone who would profoundly change my mind and bring the most loving and gentle soul into our hearts and home.

I worked part-time as an engineer for a local radio station. That evening's program featured a show about racing greyhounds and what happened once they retired.

Our guest was named *Dennis Hartman, President and Founder of a local greyhound adoption program.

The only greyhounds I knew were painted on the sides of busses or pictured on billboards. I remember my parents taking my aunt and uncle to the dog races when they visited from New Jersey. When they arrived home, Dad told of betting on a dog to win, and it was in the lead until stopping for a potty break! In my opinion, these dogs were mean and vicious. Most I've seen wore muzzles on their faces. Naively, I didn't care much about greyhounds or how they lived their lives, nor could I have imagined the story I was about to hear.

Dennis's story began with him at the dog races, unaware he was standing next to a dog owner. "Guess it's time to retire that one!" Dennis overheard the man say after witnessing his dog lose a third consecutive race. Curiously, Dennis asked the man what was going to happen next. With a stark coldness, the answer came. "I'm going to shoot him in the head!" It was then Dennis knew he had to save these majestic beings.

I was horrified to hear the many tragic stories happening with these most athletic creatures. Dogs were beaten and starved as punishment for losing races (and for costing their owners money). If it were determined an animal was of no use, it would be inhumanely tortured and destroyed. No living creature deserves this type of treatment, especially a greyhound.

I learned the ideas I held regarding greyhounds weren't true. Greyhounds are gentle and the most loving breed of dog. All they want is to please their owners and show them affection; in return, they just want to be loved. By the end of the show, I was convinced that a greyhound would be our next pet.

Excitedly arriving home, I tried explaining everything I remembered, bestowing praise and the virtues of greyhounds. After considering what happened with Oliver, Donna and I wanted to do our research. With a determined diligence, I began reading every bit of information regarding this breed. I wanted to know everything about them before deciding whether to adopt one. Armed with what I read and the information from Dennis, I was convinced a greyhound would make an ideal family pet. After discussing all the pros and we couldn't find any cons, we agreed on adopting one.

I was surprised to learn greyhounds are the only dog referred to in the Bible. In the King James version (and others), in the Book of Proverbs, greyhounds are named as one of four things stately.

Proverbs 30:29 – "There be three things that go well, yea, four are comely in going."
Proverbs 30:30 – "A lion which is strongest among beasts, and turneth not away for any."
Proverbs 30:31 – "A greyhound; an he goat also; and a king against whom there is no rising up."

When I opened my Bible, there it was in print.

The following weekend, our family drove to where Dennis kept greyhounds in search of a new home. Inside a small air-conditioned trailer, there were dogs housed in kennels, each kennel holding one dog. Every greyhound had a name and a story to tell. All were retired from racing—except for Drake, a one-year-old that never raced a day in his life. He was a big boy, a hundred pounds of solid muscle. It was hard to decide on whom we should pick. They were all worthy of taking home, but in the end, we chose Drake to come and join our family.

I was given a questionnaire asking if we would provide a suitable home along with proper food, water, and medical care for Drake. The survey seemed to ask if we were worthy or not of having him, and to sign a promise that we'd be treating him humanely. I finished filling out the paperwork, agreeing with the terms, then handed it to the person tending them. After paying the adoption fees and a neutering, we brought Drake home.

Chapter Twenty-Five

Drake Takes the Cake

HAVING A GREYHOUND is different from any other pet, as we quickly discovered. If you're looking for a big couch potato that rarely barks and is a good watchdog (he watched everything), you might need a greyhound.

In some instances, he watched a bit too much. I'm sure you've heard the expression that curiosity killed the cat; it almost killed the dog too! Drake and his nose had to investigate whatever was happening, especially in the kitchen. He could easily reach anything that wasn't attended to on the countertop, as we found out—the hard way.

Donna spent the morning making a double-layered cake for a birthday celebration happening later that day. Drake was supervising her every move, optimistically hoping for anything that might fall his way; when it didn't happen, he decided to make sure it would.

When the cakes were done baking, Donna placed them on the countertop to cool and began turning her attention to other matters. The aroma from her efforts filled every room with an inviting fragrance that was hard to ignore. Apparently, Drake thought so too. Upon her return, the cakes were GONE; not a crumb was left. If Drake had been a cat, he would have used several of his nine lives that day. So, it was time to start again, and this time, the inquisitive four-legged nose was kept away of the kitchen. The new cakes were completed in time for the celebration, with watchful eyes making sure nothing would happen to them.

Chapter Twenty-Six

CHARLOTTE AND THE DUCKS

CHARLOTTE WAS A sweetheart, an Australian Shepherd and Husky mix with eyes blue and clear as a summer's sky. She was housed at the local pound and was my Father's Day gift. Living alone, my children decided I needed a companion after my marriage ended.

The staff at this shelter worked hard making sure the adoptive owners matched well with the candidate of their choosing. After pondering over several hopeful contenders, I picked Charlotte because we seemed to bond from the moment we met.

Charlotte was found wandering in the middle of a busy street and spent her past week at the shelter. I think if Charlotte was able to speak, I would have known how appreciative she was to have a new home. Although she couldn't express herself in words, I could tell by her actions.

It was obvious she was cared for and very well mannered. Charlotte was trained unlike any other pup I'd ever known. Human food didn't interest her as she lay peacefully at my feet. I couldn't help but wonder if someone was missing her.

Charlotte was smart and seemed almost human in the way she understood my commands. When it was time to go outside, she sat patiently by the door and waited for me to escort her. Our walks were peaceful, and Charlotte was well behaved, walking calmly at my side. My naivety about trusting her behavior gave me a false sense of security. I was about to learn how quickly things can go wrong.

Florida residents share their environment with several species of wildlife that would pique the curiosity of any canine. It's not uncommon to see an iguana perched on a tree limb next to a kitchen window, or possibly an alligator catching some rays near a canal bank. That afternoon, Charlotte had her sights on something else…a group of Muscovy Ducks!

Muscovy ducks are found almost everywhere in Florida. Charlotte didn't care if they were a protected species; she was determined to get one! I parked the car after spending the day with my three offspring. Charlotte was along for the ride. My plan was to drop them off and return home with Charlotte. Before I knew it, Charlotte bolted from the car in full pursuit of several ducks standing nearby. Like a shot, she was gone! I was in hot pursuit, yelling for her to stop, but she kept on straight into a canal. When I reached the bank, she was several yards away and showing no signs of giving up her chase. My only option was to go and get her.

Stephen, Katherine, and Sarah watched anxiously as I undressed down to my undies and without hesitation dove in headfirst. The water was murky and brown. I was praying neither one of us would be on the menu for a hungry gator! This crazy pooch was determined to keep on swimming.

Eventually, she was starting to tire, and I was able to reach her. When we returned to shore, I was exhausted and surprised to see a group of spectators watching us. A few of them waded in to help pull us from the water. Once back on land, I was reminded the magnitude of danger in which I allowed myself to experience. I was appreciative and thanked them for helping me out of a bad situation.

The show was over, and everyone dispersed to what-ever they were doing before the drama began. We made our way to the apartment with Charlotte on a tightly held leash. It didn't matter if I was almost bare naked, all I needed was a hot shower and a bath for Charlotte. After we both cleaned up, Charlotte and I departed for home, thankful our circumstances didn't end with a tragedy.

Chapter Twenty-Seven
ESP–It's Not for Me

THERE WAS NOTHING out of the ordinary that Saturday afternoon. Our family spent an enjoyable visit with my dad's parents. When it was time to go, we said our good-byes and left for home. It wasn't long after our departure that I began to feel uneasy and saw a snapshot glimpse of a vision. As bad as this may sound, I saw my grandfather's body laid out in his casket! For some unexplained reason, this foretelling sight chose me to be its messenger. Absolutely nothing could have alerted or prepared me for what was to come.

There are times when it's best to keep your thoughts hidden and not let them escape into the universe. This was one of those times. I spoke up and mentioned what I'd just visualized, not expecting the response that came in return. Harsh words of criticism from both sides of the front seat, where my parents were sitting, came hurling toward me. The mood was tense. I was embarrassed and ashamed for speaking my mind. Sitting quietly, I was afraid to utter another sound for the remainder of the trip.

By the time we arrived home, tensions had settled, and normal family activities resumed. I tried to forget about that terrible sight and the chastising I received. The next morning, as usual, we attended church. Arriving home, we heard the phone ringing as we entered through the front door. My grandmother was calling to inform us that Big Daddy was on the ICU floor at a local hospital after suffering a heart attack earlier that morning. Dad left immediately for the hospital, while Mom stayed home with Becky and me.

Feelings of intense guilt started to overwhelm me as I began thinking it was my fault our grandfather was lying in the hospital. I wanted to go back and erase the image and my words as if they had never happened. My guilty feelings were intensified even more after hearing news of his passing. As a rational adult, one might say this was a mere coincidence, but do coincidences really happen? My belief is yes, and they can happen at any time. It took a while before I convinced myself the two events were not related. I couldn't help but wonder if my parents held any resentment toward me for sharing what I'd seen. If they did, I never knew it.

Chapter Twenty-Eight

HELLO...IS ANYBODY THERE?

GROWING UP, I was led to believe that ghosts were the product of an overactive imagination. If that were true, there must be logical answers to the unexplained events I've encountered. I seem to have a heightened awareness and a sensitivity to things in which I can't explain. I first noticed these odd occurrences happening while working at a local TV station. Most of my time there was overnight and alone, or so I thought. Many times, I wondered if that were true. Squeaking doors followed by approaching footsteps were the normal experiences on my watch. The steps became louder as they grew closer. Seated at my desk, I would be expecting someone to enter through the doorway when, suddenly, there would be total silence. I would rise from my chair to investigate, and nobody would be there. Occasionally, I would feel an ominous "presence" in the room and detect the aroma of a woman's perfume. I tried to ignore many of the things that were happening, while keeping a vigil on my work.

I was notified by station management that a mandatory staff meeting was being held on a Friday afternoon. All employees were expected to attend with no exceptions.

After the meeting, I approached my supervisor and asked if he was aware of any strange happenings at the station. His answer didn't provide much comfort when he asked me if I was hearing them too. Shortly afterwards, I took on a new role with a different company, hoping to leave these strange encounters behind. Unfortunately, it was not to be. There would be more eerie events to come.

I noticed these unusual things happened frequently when there were high levels of EMF or Electrical Magnetic Force in the area. Maybe that would explain all the activity occurring at the TV station. My hypothesis seemed to have some merit when I began working as a security officer at an electric power plant. What I had witnessed previously was tame in comparison. These new entities were about to step up their game.

For some reason, people shy away from mentioning anything that might seem crazy—that is, until something unexplainable happens. I'd been working at the power plant a few weeks when I learned about a strange event that left a co-worker shaken.

Sherry was a security officer and night auditor working alone in a small area with limited space. A full-sized office copier sat to the right of two desks configured at a 90-degree angle. Most of the attention was focused toward the front entrance and away from the copier. When it was time to print copies, Sherry was shocked to see the huge machine had moved from where it had been installed to the middle of the floor. It might have gone farther if not for an electrical cord holding it firmly to the wall. After gaining her composure, Sherry managed to move the copier back in place, and nothing out of the ordinary occurred for the remainder of the night. Unfortunately, the same incident happened again with another co-worker, leaving her just as upset. Although not an eyewitness to the two copier incidents, I was an unwilling participant when things became physical.

It started as a typical evening in the same cramped area. With my favorite station providing background music, I began working. Suddenly, the tranquility was interrupted by a loud crashing noise. I was convinced the storage shelves in the adjacent room had collapsed! Much to my astonishment, NOTHING was disturbed! My immediate reaction was to leave. Since that was not an option, I continued working with a heightened level of anxiety.

Sherry arrived for work and didn't seem surprised to hear of my harrowing experience. "Oh, that happens all the time; it's nothing to worry about." Her statement wasn't helping to put me at ease. I can handle dealing with squeaky doors and approaching footsteps; loud crashes that seemingly didn't happen are harder to accept.

These poltergeists were about to show me a whole new level of pranking. Most of the time, the windows in our work area remained closed in order to keep the heat or cooled air from escaping. On rare occasions, with weather permitting, the windows were opened to catch a refreshing breeze.

The summer heat was ablaze as I stepped from my car. It was a short stroll to the security entrance. I felt a refreshing rush of cold air greet me as I entered through the doorway. Speaking briefly with the guard on duty, I noticed something was missing from its place. A large bowl that had sat undisturbed for months had disappeared.

When I inquired as to the whereabouts of the bowl, I was told the ghost had removed it from the shelf. I nervously laughed it off, hoping it wasn't true.

The bowl was sitting on top of a file cabinet near the shelf where it had previously rested. Testing fate, I wanted to see if this type of thing could really happen. I removed the bowl from the file cabinet and placed it back on the shelf, then waited for something to happen.

Keeping my focus on work assignments and away from ghostly ventures was difficult. The thought of a bowl mysteriously falling off a shelf by itself was unsettling to me. I began trying to rationalize that maybe it was too close to the edge and a gust of wind blew it to the floor. That scenario didn't work because all the windows were securely closed! Maybe there was a logical reason—it just fell. I was trying hard to convince myself this was a once-in-a-lifetime event never to happen again. Several hours passed with the bowl not budging an inch. I was growing more confident that my theory was correct, almost daring it to move. My overzealous thoughts were about to change rapidly.

A wise person once quoted that sleeping dogs should remain undisturbed—you might want to add cantankerous spirits to the list. After an uneventful evening, my shift would soon be ending. I was finishing up with my work in preparation for the next officer's arrival. In an instant and without warning, my peaceful environment was destroyed. Immediately, I knew what had transpired. The bowl was missing from the shelf and spinning on the floor like a top! I calmly walked to the spot where the bowl had landed and placed it back on the file cabinet. I wasn't about to tempt fate again.

I believe the spiritual world does exist. Too many things convince me to believe otherwise. Strange encounters, such as the one happening the night Dad passed away, are intriguing. Mom was alone in her room lying face down across the bed, arms extended above her head. Suddenly feeling as if someone was gripping her hands, Mom raised up, thinking our pastor had entered the room, and nobody was there. I'm firmly convinced it was Dad letting her know that he was doing okay.

Chapter Twenty-Nine

THE TALE END

ON THE NIGHT of our high school commencement The Road Less Traveled by Robert Frost was read to our graduating class. Afterwards there were hugs and tears as we said our goodbyes and went our separate ways ready to take on the world. Some of us would begin college or start on their careers; others would join the military.

My journey has taken me on a road traveled by many generations. The unpredictability of not knowing what lies ahead reminds me that tomorrow is never promised. I am grateful for my soulmate Barbara and the many blessings that have been bestowed upon me.

When I decided to take my thoughts to paper, I wasn't sure where to start, the words just began appearing on the screen as if someone was typing them for me. I give praise to my Heavenly Father for without him these words could not have been scribed. There were times when sheer determination kept me going when every written word was lost. After starting from the beginning for the third time I decided it was time to back up my work. Maybe it was a good thing because the third time is supposed to be a charm.

Although my life began in a critical state I managed to survive. Becky and I were raised by two loving parents that furnished all of our needs in a comfortable middle-class home. I didn't truly appreciate our parent's sacrifices until it was too late to let them know. I am who I am because of who they were and the values they instilled in me.

As a young boy I remember our mom telling us stories and quoting lines she'd read in books written by Erma Bombeck, a popular American humorist during the 1960's through the mid 1990's. Those stories helped to plant seeds in my imagination and for the first time I believed I could become a writer.

Growing up I was shy with very little self-confidence, and never dated during high school. Despite that, I had an alter ego trying to escape. When I discovered I could get people to laugh it helped to bring me out of my shyness. It let me feel accepted. Having my own radio program also helped. Anonymously hiding behind a microphone gave me confidence and was much easier than facing someone in person. I didn't worry if people were judging me, all that mattered was keeping my station manager happy.

I am grateful for having been blessed with you as my children. I cannot think of any better gift than sharing my past with you. My wish is that my words will live on in your hearts long after I'm gone. Your mom and I did our best to prepare you in bringing our family's legacy forward. I know you will succeed in doing so.

Love, Dad.

CPSIA information can be obtained
at www.ICGtesting.com
Printed in the USA
LVHW110013030422
714933LV00020B/625